Edexcel GCSE Music Exam

The Essential Knowledge Organiser

Robert Legg

2023 EDITION

A Challis-Baker Book

Edexcel GCSE Music Exam: The Essential Knowledge Organiser

2023 EDITION

ISBN 978-1-7392847-0-1

Copyright © Robert Legg 2023

A Challis-Baker Book published in Oxford, United Kingdom

All rights reserved

Cover design by Saroj Prajapati.

Acknowledgements. The following images are in the public domain or are used with permission. **Brandenburg Concerto**. Image of autograph manuscript: Staatsbibliothek zu Berlin, 1721. Image of harpsichord: Toshiyuki IMAI, 2008. **Pathétique Sonata**. Image of piano hammers: Jan Fidler, 2013. Image of first edition facsimile: Beethoven-Haus, Bonn, 1800. Karl Joseph Stieler's portrait of Beethoven: Beethoven-Haus, Bonn, 1820. **Music for a While**. Jean-Auguste-Dominique Ingres's Oedipus and the Sphynx: Art Gallery ErgSat, c. 1826. Image of viols by Christopher Simpson: Cyclocifra, 2007. John Closterman's portrait of Purcell, 1695. **Killer Queen**. Freddie Mercury image: Carl Lender, 2014. Instrument images reproduced with permission. Image of Freddie Mercury's signature: Angelus for Wikimedia, 2011. **Defying Gravity**. Illustrated front cover to first edition of L. Frank Baum's The Wonderful Wizard of Oz: W. W. Denslow, 1900. Wicked billboard in Times Square image: Glen Scarborough, 2009. Stephen Schwartz image: Nathan Johnson for stephenschwartz.com, 2022, reproduced with permission. **Star Wars**. Star Wars orchestral concert image: Steven Miller, 2010. John Williams image: TashTish, 2007. **Afro Celt Sound System**. Instrument images reproduced with permission. Image of N'Faly Kouyate: Brian Marks, 2007. Image of Sinéad O'Connor: Phil King, 2012, for Man Alive! **Samba Em Prelúdio**. Esperanza Spalding image: Andrea Mancini, 2009. Roberto Baden Powell image: Philippe Baden Powell, 1971.

Every effort has been made to trace copyright holders and to obtain their permission for the use of copyright material. The author apologises for any errors or omissions in the above list and would be grateful if notified of any corrections that should be incorporated in future reprints or editions of this book.

This book is not written, published, approved or endorsed by Edexcel or Pearson plc. Please check the up-to-date Edexcel specification, since this is liable to change. The author has used his best efforts to ensure the accuracy of the information in this guide, but does not assume any liability for errors or omissions it may contain.

Contents

Area of Study 1: INSTRUMENTAL MUSIC 1700-1820

Bach: Brandenburg Concerto no. 5 in D major: third movement 4

Beethoven: Piano Sonata no. 8 in C min Op. 13, 'Pathétique' (first movement) 8

Area of Study 2: VOCAL MUSIC

Purcell: 'Music for a While' 12

'Killer Queen' from Queen's album Sheer Heart Attack (1974) 16

Area of Study 3: MUSIC FOR STAGE AND SCREEN

Schwartz: 'Defying Gravity' from Wicked (2003) 20

John Williams: 'Main Title' / 'Rebel Blockade Runner' from Star Wars (1977) 24

Area of Study 4: FUSIONS

'Release' (from Volume 2: Release) by Afro Celt Sound System 28

'Samba Em Prelúdio' performed by Esperanza Spalding 32

Bach: Brandenburg Concerto no. 5 in D major: third movement

LESSON 1

Who Was BACH?

Really important **GERMAN** composer of the **BAROQUE PERIOD**. Chosen here so that you can show you know about **BAROQUE FEATURES** and the **CONCERTO GROSSO**.

When Was This Written?

Composed in **1720/1**, this is a concerto of the later part of the **BAROQUE ERA**, 1600-1750.

Who's in the Spotlight?

Watch out for the Italian names of the instruments on this score! You need to know that the three **SOLO** instruments are:

(1) a **FLUTE** ("flauto")

(2) a **VIOLIN** ("violin principale") and

(3) a **HARPSICHORD** ("cembalo concertato").

All three of these parts are written to be quite **VIRTUOSIC**, which means that they are difficult to play and impressive to hear performed.

Who's the Back-Up?

The players in the accompanying orchestra are **VIOLINS** ("violino di ripieno"), **VIOLAS** ("viola da ripieno"), **CELLOS** ("violoncello") and an instrument called a **VIOLONE** which is an early double-bass type of instrument, here labelled "contrabasso" on the score.

These parts are much less **VIRTUOSIC**, which means that they are easier.

What's the Structure?

ABA or **TERNARY**. Sections as follows:

SECTION A (bars 1-78) is in D major and is **FUGATO**. Fugato means it has lots of **IMITATION**, like a fugue.

SECTION B (bars 79-232) is in B minor and is a **RITORNELLO**. Ritornello means that the same little bits of melody from SECTION A keep coming back.

SECTION A returns (bars 233-310).

The Essential Knowledge Organiser

What is a CONCERTO?

A three-movement piece for solo instrument(s) and orchestra. In a CONCERTO GROSSO, like this one, there is more than one solo instrument.

CONCERTINO
is the name of the small group of solo (lead) instruments.

RIPIENO
is the group of accompanying instruments.

What BAROQUE FEATURES are heard in this piece?

This work is packed full of characteristic BAROQUE FEATURES. Here's the checklist:

- ☑ Melodic features like SEQUENCE and IMITATION.
- ☑ Use of BASSO CONTINUO.
- ☑ Lots of ORNAMENTATION.
- ☑ Long, flowing melodies.
- ☑ POLYPHONIC texture.
- ☑ Limited dynamic range. (TERRACED DYNAMICS rather than gradual changes.)
- ☑ Harmonic features like PEDAL NOTES and SUSPENSIONS.
- ☑ Clear, DIATONIC harmony.
- ☑ Use of a DANCE form.
- ☑ Baroque INSTRUMENTS like the HARPSICHORD and VIOLONE.

What's That About This Being a BAROQUE DANCE FORM?

This piece is a JIG (also spelled "gigue").

How do we know? It's lively, and it's got two main beats in the bar. Each beat is divided into three little beats. This is called COMPOUND DUPLE. It's usually expressed as 6/8, but here it's in 2/4 with triplets indicated throughout.

What's that HARPSICHORD doing?

The HARPSICHORD is an early (old-fashioned) keyboard instrument. It's like a piano but the strings are mechanically plucked, so it can't do dynamics. Here, the harpsichord is part of the CONCERTINO, so it often plays a VIRTUOSIC solo line. When it's not doing that, it plays a BASSO CONTINUO line. In these sections, the player uses the tiny numbers under the music of the bass line ("FIGURED BASS") to work out which notes to play. The VIOLONE is also part of the CONTINUO, playing the bass line too.

Edexcel GCSE Music Exam

Bach: Brandenburg Concerto no. 5 in D major: third movement
LESSON 2

What Can We Say About TEXTURE?

Long story short, this piece is **POLYPHONIC**. This means it uses multiple, interweaving tunes or lines, each playing different rhythms. There are some exceptions to this basic rule.

Strictly speaking, the opening of the movement is ← **MONOPHONIC**, since there is a single line playing unaccompanied (bars 1 and 2).

Strictly speaking, some moments are briefly **HOMOPHONIC** → since all the parts all move together in the same basic rhythm (e.g. bars 46 and 47).

Most of the writing, however, is **POLYPHONIC**, using interweaving and overlapping tunes or lines. The texture often uses **IMITATION**. *These are your go-to answers to texture questions on this work!*

How Do I Know This Is BAROQUE?

This question, or a variation on it, is quite likely to be asked. Pretty much *everything* on this page can be used in your answer! Just add "... which is a characteristic feature of the Baroque Era" to any description.

"The texture is mainly **polyphonic** → which is a characteristic feature of the Baroque Era."

"There are **pedal notes** and **clear perfect cadences** → which are characteristic harmonic features of the Baroque Era."

"The melody contains **sequences** and uses **imitation** → which are characteristic melodic features of the Baroque Era."

"The composer uses **ornamentation** → which is a characteristic melodic feature of the Baroque Era."

"The melody has **dance-like elements** (dotted rhythms and triplets) → which are characteristic features of the Baroque Era."

What ORNAMENTS Are Used?

Only two kinds are used in this work:

TRILL (marked *tr* in the score), which is when the player alternates the note written with the note above, rapidly.

APPOGGIATURA (a tiny note written in before the main note), which is an extra note *not* in the chord, added to create harmonic interest. (See bar 90 in the violin for an example.)

What About the INSTRUMENTS?

Make sure you know all the instruments listed on p. 4. Don't forget to call the harpsichord line **VIRTUOSIC** if you get half a chance.

The Essential Knowledge Organiser

What If I'm Asked to Describe/Compare the HARMONIC FEATURES?

First, remember that this uses the DIATONIC harmonies of the BAROQUE ERA. That means the piece has a clear major/minor key (D major then B minor) and chords chosen from within that key.

PEDAL NOTES are a really important feature, especially in Section B. These are long, held low notes, which have changing chords above them. (Look at the bass line here, ← bars 81 to 83.)

Each main section ends with a clear PERFECT CADENCE. → Section A finishes in D major, Section B in B minor. Look at the bass line in this example.

In addition to these features, Bach sometimes uses SUSPENSIONS and APPOGGIATURAS to create interest. Don't worry too much about these: DIATONIC HARMONIES, PEDAL NOTES and PERFECT CADENCES are your go-to answers to questions about the HARMONIC FEATURES of this work!

And What If I'm Asked to Describe/Compare a MELODY (or the MELODIC FEATURES)?

The SUBJECT (main tune) of Section A has a number of key features. You might need to describe them:

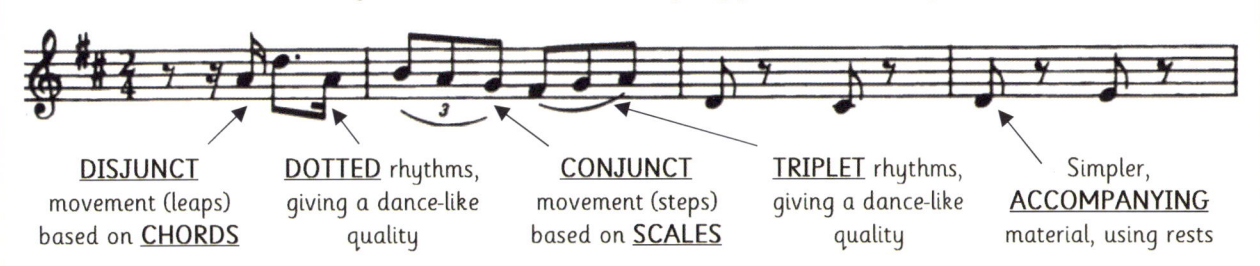

DISJUNCT movement (leaps) based on **CHORDS**

DOTTED rhythms, giving a dance-like quality

CONJUNCT movement (steps) based on **SCALES**

TRIPLET rhythms, giving a dance-like quality

Simpler, **ACCOMPANYING** material, using rests

SEQUENCE, where part of a tune is repeated up or down a note, often more than once, is a main feature here. When it's repeated up a note, it's an ASCENDING SEQUENCE. Down a note, a DESCENDING SEQUENCE. ↓

(ASCENDING SEQUENCE in solo violin, bars 102-104)

↑ IMITATION is a major feature of the melodic writing. This is where one instrument copies another. Here the flute IMITATES (copies) the violin at the opening of the movement.

Your go-to answers about the MELODIC FEATURES of this work are SEQUENCE, IMITATION, and DOTTED and TRIPLET RHYTHMS. See also the ORNAMENTATION panel on page 6.

Edexcel GCSE Music Exam

Beethoven: Piano Sonata no. 8 in C min Op. 13, 'Pathétique': first movement

LESSON 3

Who Was BEETHOVEN?

Really important GERMAN composer of the late CLASSICAL PERIOD. Chosen here so you can show what you know about the CLASSICAL STYLE, the early ROMANTIC STYLE and about PIANO WRITING.

Moving from Classical to Romantic

Published in 1799, this is a sonata of the CLASSICAL ERA, 1750-1820. However, it also contains some ROMANTIC ERA elements. You need to know about both "sides" of this piece.

MOOD

This piece is known for its TRAGIC and EMOTIONALLY EXPRESSIVE mood, hence the nickname 'Pathétique', which refers to the idea of SUFFERING.

Written For a NEW INSTRUMENT

This sonata shows what the new(ish) "PIANOFORTE" could do that a harpsichord couldn't:

- ☑ Wide DYNAMIC range and gradual changes (crescendo).
- ☑ Long, SUSTAINED notes that don't die away quickly.
- ☑ Wide COMPASS, allowing LONG DESCENTS, WIDE LEAPS and CONTRASTING REGISTERS.
- ☑ Different ACCENTS and ARTICULATIONS (e.g. sf)
- ☑ Allowed the performer to display great VIRTUOSITY.

How About TONALITY, HARMONY and TEXTURE?

In summary, the piece is in C MINOR.

Harmonically, it's generally SIMPLE (in line with Classical Style). Interesting features are the DRAMATIC DIMINISHED SEVENTH CHORDS and the modulation to UNUSUAL KEYS.

The texture is always HOMOPHONIC. Sometimes this is tune-and-accompaniment, sometimes just chords. But *always* HOMOPHONIC!

What is a SONATA?

A SONATA is a composition for solo instrument, usually in three or four movements. Sometimes sonatas feature a piano accompaniment, when the solo instrument isn't the piano, e.g. you could have a sonata for cello and piano.

BE CAREFUL! A SONATA and SONATA FORM are different things. For this set work, you need both terms: it's a SONATA FORM MOVEMENT which is part of a three-movement SONATA written for piano.

What's the STRUCTURE?

This is a SONATA FORM MOVEMENT. See the next page for more detail on the structure.

SLOW INTRODUCTION

(bars 1 to 10)

EXPOSITION

(bars 11 to 132)

DEVELOPMENT

(bars 133 to 194)

RECAPITULATION

(bars 195 to end)

What CLASSICAL FEATURES are heard in this piece?

This work displays characteristic features of the CLASSICAL STYLE. Here's the checklist:

- ☑ Use of the established SONATA FORM structure.
- ☑ Elegant, BALANCED PHRASES also called PERIODIC PHRASING.
- ☑ Use of ALBERTI BASS to sustain the notes of a chord.
- ☑ Light HOMOPHONIC textures.

What ROMANTIC FEATURES are heard in this piece?

The work *also* shows characteristic features of the ROMANTIC ERA. Here's the checklist:

- ☑ DEVELOPMENTS to the established SONATA FORM structure, e.g. the slow introduction.
- ☑ Violent EMOTIONS.
- ☑ Extreme contrasts of DYNAMICS.
- ☑ Unusual choice of KEYS for the different sections of the piece.

Beethoven: Piano Sonata no. 8 in C min Op. 13, 'Pathétique': first movement

LESSON 4

How Does It Start?

With a **SLOW INTRODUCTION** (bars 1-10):

Is It Nearly Finished?

No. It's the **DEVELOPMENT SECTION**, kicking off with an idea from the intro (from bar 133):

Then what? Then Beethoven plays around with fragments of the themes from the Exposition.

It's a free-for-all, basically.

Don't get too worried about it. But you need to know that at bar 167 he starts to prepare for the next section with a thirty-bar **DOMINANT PREPARATION**:

Look out for the **DOMINANT PEDAL** at the very the bottom of the texture. It lasts for thirty bars! If you get the chance to mention that, do!

Then There's an EXPOSITION, right?

Yes. It's got a **FIRST SUBJECT** (from bar 11)

then a **SECOND SUBJECT** appearing first in the 'wrong' key of Eb minor (bar 51)

before settling into the expected Eb major at bar 89. Then you've got a codetta, which references the **FIRST SUBJECT** (bar 121).

Usually the **EXPOSITION** is repeated.

Do I REALLY Need to Know All This?

Well, the main points here are that Beethoven writes in an established **SONATA FORM**:

(Intro)–EXPOSITION–DEVELOPMENT–RECAPITULATION

But then plays around with the way the material appears in different keys.

Do you have some words to DESCRIBE the MELODIES used in this piece?

What ORNAMENTS Are Used?

TRILL (marked *tr* in the score), which is when the player alternates the note written with the note above, rapidly.

ACCIACCIATURA (a tiny note with a slash through it written in before the main note), which is a 'grace note' played quickly to decorate the melody.

MORDENT (looks like a tiny mountain range), which means you play the printed note, the note above, and the printed note again. Normally you do this quite quickly.

What's the METRE?

C = 4/4 = SIMPLE QUADRUPLE
C with a vertical line = 2/2 = SIMPLE DUPLE

Just the RECAPITULATION to go?

Yes. The FIRST SUBJECT returns (bar 195)

then the SECOND SUBJECT comes back first in the 'wrong' key of F minor (bar 221)

before settling into the expected C minor. Then you've got the CODA, which references the INTRO and FIRST SUBJECT. The End.

Good Thing to Mention #1
This has CLASSICAL and ROMANTIC elements. Be ready to list some of each.

Good Thing to Mention #2
Beethoven is showing off the capability of the NEW PIANO. Do you know how?

Good Thing to Mention #3
This is a SONATA FORM MOVEMENT. It has three sections. (*Don't say ternary or ABA.*)

Good Thing to Mention #4
Beethoven makes CHANGES to the normal sonata form structure. Mainly with KEYS.

Good Thing to Mention #5
The piano writing is VIRTUOSIC. Be ready to give some examples of flashy writing.

Good Thing to Mention #6
HARMONIC devices include DIMINISHED SEVENTH CHORDS and PEDAL NOTES.

Good Thing to Mention #7
It's about SUFFERING! Talk about the EXTREME DYNAMICS and MINOR KEY.

Good Thing to Mention #8
The piece includes many big CONTRASTS including tempo, range, texture.

The Essential Knowledge Organiser

Edexcel GCSE Music Exam

Purcell: 'Music for a While'

LESSON 5

SOPRANO?!

Originally written for **TENOR**, actually.

Who Was HENRY PURCELL?

An important English composer of the 1600s. Purcell wrote music for the church, the stage and many royal occasions. This song was **INCIDENTAL MUSIC** for a play called *Oedipus*.

Is This a LAMENT? (Yes, It Is.)

- ☑ Does it have a lot of **FALLING PHRASES**?
- ☑ Is it in a **MINOR KEY**?
- ☑ Does it move at a **SLOW TEMPO**?

Then it's a LAMENT!

What's the TEXTURE?

Always **HOMOPHONIC**, because there's always a clear tune with an accompaniment. The accompanying bass line is more active that some others, because it's a **GROUND BASS**. Nevertheless, *your go-to answer about texture here is that it's* **HOMOPHONIC**.

What BAROQUE FEATURES are heard in this piece?

This work is packed full of characteristic **BAROQUE FEATURES**. Here's the checklist:

- ☑ Melodic **SEQUENCES**.
- ☑ Use of **BASSO CONTINUO**.
- ☑ Use of a **GROUND BASS**.
- ☑ Use of **ORNAMENTATION**.
- ☑ Long, flowing melodies.
- ☑ Use of **WORD-PAINTING**.
- ☑ **HOMOPHONIC** texture.
- ☑ Limited dynamic range. (**TERRACED DYNAMICS** rather than gradual changes.)
- ☑ Harmonic features like **SUSPENSIONS**.
- ☑ Clear, **DIATONIC** harmony.
- ☑ Use of a **DANCE** form.
- ☑ Baroque **INSTRUMENTS** like the **HARPSICHORD** and **BASS VIOL**.

FIGURED BASS!? (BASSO CONTINUO)

Back in the Baroque Era, composers cut their workload by only writing the bass line, not the full accompaniment.

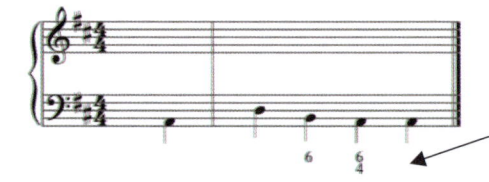

The players used the tiny figures under the notes to work out the rest for themselves!

The Essential Knowledge Organiser

Who's Playing What?

SOPRANO singer. Sings the tune and words. Is allowed to add ornaments, especially to A¹.

HARPSICHORD. Early (old-fashioned) keyboard instrument. Plays the bass line and uses the FIGURED BASS to improvise a full accompaniment.

BASS VIOL. Just plays the bass line, adding extra weight/tone.

Forma Chelyos utravis Minuritonibus apta, sed Prima resonantior.

The Figure or Shape of a Division-Viol may be either of these; but the First is better for Sound.

But there aren't any tiny FIGURES on the score...

Well, no. Purcell didn't *even* put figures on this bass line. So, it was *completely* up to the player how to play it. Luckily, the shape of the bass line strongly implies chords in most places.

What's the Structure?

There are two key points to make here. First, the overall structure is ABA¹ (TERNARY) form:

INSTRUMENTAL INTRODUCTION (bar 1 to bar 3) A minor
SECTION A "Music, music for a while ..." (bar 4 to bar 15) A minor → E minor
SECTION B "Till Alecto ..." (bar 16 to 28) G → different modulations → A minor
SECTION A¹ "Music, music for a while ..." (bar 29 to end) A minor

The second important point is that the piece is a GROUND BASS, which means that it has a repeating bassline. Here the GROUND BASS is three bars long:

Note how the first notes of each group of four climb from the tonic note, A, to the dominant note, E.

The GROUND BASS is heard TWELVE TIMES throughout the piece, although some of the middle versions are adapted to allow different harmonies to be played over it.

The GROUND BASS is a characteristic feature of the BAROQUE ERA and was often used by PURCELL.

Purcell: 'Music for a While'

LESSON 6

Just Four Examples of WORD-PAINTING

"all, all ... all, all" — Bars 7 to 9. This word is REPEATED, giving the idea of many, many cares or troubles.

"pains" — Bar 12. Strong DISCORD created by a SUSPENSION. E and D clash against each other powerfully.

"eternal" — Bars 19 to 21. Long MELSIMA used on this word, indicating the everlasting nature of death.

"drop, drop ... drop, drop" — Bars 23-25. Repeated notes, sung off the beat, in a somewhat chaotic line, suggest the idea of snakes dropping.

Some More Things About WORD-SETTING and VOCAL LINE

Most of the time, Purcell uses a <u>SYLLABIC</u> setting (using one note per syllable), which retains the speech-like quality of the words and makes them easy to understand.

Sometimes, however, he emphasises a word with a <u>MELISMATIC</u> setting. For example, 'eternal' (as described above) is set on a melisma to emphasise the meaning of that word. Similarly, 'wond'ring' is set to a melisma, to emphasise the idea of unhurried contemplation and thoughtfulness.

The melodic line moves in a <u>CONJUNCT</u> (stepwise) way, with the occasional <u>DISJUNCT</u> movement (leap). It contains <u>SEQUENCES</u>.

All these points help keep the song <u>DIRECT</u>, <u>DRAMATIC</u> and <u>EASY TO UNDERSTAND</u>.

ORNAMENTS

UPPER MORDENT

Play/sing the note written, the note *above*, the note written again.

LOWER MORDENT

Play/sing the note written, the note *below*, the note written again.

APPOGGIATURA

A tiny note written in before the main note, as an extra note *not* in the chord, added to create harmonic interest.

GRACE NOTES

Extra non-chord notes, in, for example, bar 6.

TRILLS

Rapidly alternate the note written with the note above.

ARPEGGIATION

Notes of the chord are spread out like an arpeggio (see last bar of harpsichord part).

The Essential Knowledge Organiser

What's the METRE?

4/4 = SIMPLE QUADRUPLE

What Are the DYNAMICS?

None indicated. This is in keeping with the tradition of the time. It was left up to the performers to decide.

ANTICIPATION … IMITATION

Sometimes the improvised harpsichord part briefly anticipates the singer's written line. See bar 9, for example.

SUSPENSIONS

Sometimes Purcell creates DISSONANCE (a clash) by carrying a note from a previous chord into the next chord, where it clashes with the 'real' notes of that chord. This is called a SUSPENSION.

Be Sure to Say … #1

This piece has loads of BAROQUE ERA fingerprints. Make sure you know them all.

Be Sure to Say … #2

It's not just in a minor key and a sad mood. It's a LAMENT! Don't forget to say so!

Be Sure to Say … #3

You *must* say it's based on a GROUND BASS. Then *add* that it's in ternary form.

Be Sure to Say … #4

Purcell emphasises the TEXT: word-painting, and the syllabic, conjunct setting.

Be Sure to Say … #5

Lots of things are LEFT UP TO THE PERFORMERS: dynamics, accompaniment.

Be Sure to Say … #6

Main HARMONIC device (GROUND BASS aside) is use of SUSPENSIONS.

Be Sure to Say … #7

Melodic features include ORNAMENTS, SEQUENCES and WORD-PAINTING.

Edexcel GCSE Music Exam

'Killer Queen' from Queen's 1974 album *Sheer Heart Attack*

LESSON 7

What's This Song About?

The lyric refers to a high-class prostitute, who enjoys the finer things in life – Moët et Chandon champagne, Parisian perfume, caviar, etc. – but who provides 'mind-blowing' services, distracting her clients from 'Khrushchev and Kennedy', the political concerns of the day.

What Was 'QUEEN'?

<u>GLAM ROCK</u> group formed in 1970 in London. Known for its breadth of musical styles, <u>CLOSE HARMONY</u> and use of <u>OVERDUBBING</u>.

What <u>GUITAR TECHNIQUES</u> are heard in this piece?

<u>Distortion</u> = see the Music Technology panel (on p. 17).

<u>Wah-wah</u> = a pedal that creates an effect a bit like a human voice going "wah wah", hence the name.

<u>String bend</u> = an expressive technique where the string is pulled up or pushed down to increase the pitch.

<u>Slide</u> = using a metal tool to slide between frets, creating a glissando effect.

<u>Pull-offs</u> = a technique where the string is released forcefully, allowing a second note to sound afterwards.

<u>Vibrato</u> = a technique where the string is pushed up and down rapidly to create fluctuations in the pitch.

Freddie Mercury

Freddie Mercury was Queen's charismatic <u>LEAD SINGER</u> and <u>PIANIST</u>. He was born in 1946 in Zanzibar and went to school in India. He died of AIDS-related complications in 1991.

INFLUENCES on Queen

Queen's basic musical genre is usually described as <u>GLAM ROCK</u>, a 1970s style known for being <u>CAMP</u>, and for its <u>OUTRAGEOUS COSTUMES</u>. Other influences on Queen included:

<u>VAUDEVILLE</u> = a very popular form of light entertainment with comedy elements involving singing, dancing and acting.

<u>GOSPEL</u> = African-American musical tradition of religious singing in rich harmonies.

<u>MUSICAL THEATRE</u>

What's The STRUCTURE?

'Killer Queen' has a VERSE-CHORUS structure.

Verse 1 — "She keeps a Moet et Chandon …"
Chorus — "She's a killer queen …"
Short Instrumental
Verse 2 — "To avoid complications …"
Chorus — "She's a killer queen …"
Instrumental with Guitar Solo
Verse 3 — "Drop of a hat …"
Chorus — "She's a killer queen …"
Outro and Fade — "You wanna try …?"

What MUSIC TECHNOLOGY is heard in this piece?

Overdubbing = recording and then recording again on top of the original.

Distortion = setting the level of an electronic instrument to go 'too high' to create a 'gritty' sound.

Reverb = artificial effect of a boomy or echoey acoustic.

Panning = using stereo recording to place an instrument more to one speaker (or headphone) than the other.

Flanging = an effect that creates an other-worldly swooshing sound (used for WORD-PAINTING on 'LASER BEAM').

A Sound Created By OVERDUBBING

Of the effects mentioned above, OVERDUBBING is the most important.

BRIAN MAY plays all the guitar lines in the recording, each OVERDUBBED onto the track, to create Queen's GUITAR SOUND.

FREDDIE MERCURY does the same with the impressive FOUR-PART VOCALS.

Queen's INSTRUMENTS (and don't forget that there is NO SYNTHESIZER!)

- Vocals
- Piano 
- Electric guitar 
- Bass guitar 
- 'Jangle' piano 
- Drum kit and percussion

Edexcel GCSE Music Exam

'Killer Queen' from Queen's 1974 album *Sheer Heart Attack*

LESSON 8

What's the TONALITY?

Mainly in E flat major – which was a very unusual key for a rock song of its time.

There are lots of MODULATIONS (changes of key). Again, this is unusual.

What TEXTURES Are Used?

The texture is HOMOPHONIC because it is always a tune with an accompaniment.

The texture of the accompaniment varies from LIGHT (at the start) to DENSE (at various points).

There are very short POLYPHONIC MOMENTS where the guitar imitates the vocal line. For example, in bar 62, "willing as" is imitated in the guitar parts.

What are the main features of the VOCAL WRITING in 'Killer Queen'?

Here's the checklist:

- ☑ Mainly SYLLABIC setting.
- ☑ Each verse and each chorus begin with a little PICK-UP (or ANACRUSIS). (For example, in "To a-VOID complications" the first two syllables are the pick-up.)
- ☑ MASSIVE RANGE of two 8ves and a 3rd!
- ☑ Four-part harmonies created by OVERDUBBING Freddy Mercury's voice.
- ☑ Slides (PORTAMENTO) are used on some words, e.g. the word 'Queen' in bar 15.
- ☑ Some MELODIC SEQUENCES are used. For example, "Caviar and cigarettes" (bar 12) → "well versed in etiquette" (bar 13).

RHYTHMS

SYNCOPATION is a very important feature of the rhythms used in 'Killer Queen'. This is where the important syllables of the tune fall on the off-beats rather than the strong beats.

The rhythm used on 'just like Marie Antoinette' becomes an important MOTIF throughout the entire song:

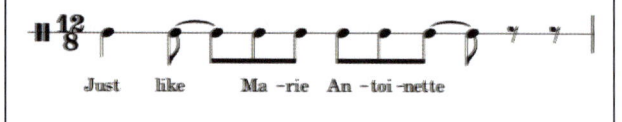

[musical notation in 12/8: Just like Ma-rie An-toi-nette]

[Freddie Mercury signature]

What *Doesn't* the GUITAR Ever Do?

There's never any STRUMMING!

HARMONIES

Two important things to mention here:

CIRCLE OF FIFTHS progression, where each chord becomes the dominant of the next. Bars 20 and 21. (A-Dm-G^7-C)

EXTENDED CHORDS, where extra notes are added to create harmonic interest. A device influenced by jazz harmonies. B♭^{11}, F^{11}, etc.

What INDICATIONS Are Used?

Vibrato symbol. ↑

8va - - - - -

Played an octave higher. ↑

Pitch bend lines. ↑

P.M. = Palm mute.

LOPSIDED Phrases

The audience's interest is maintained with a few SURPRISES.

The 6/8 bar (bar 10) comes as a LOPSIDED surprise.

The CHORUS has a 5-BAR PHRASE followed by a 3-BAR PHRASE. Again, this keeps the audience listening and comes as a surprise.

What's the METRE?

There are clearly FOUR BEATS in each bar.

This means it's in some kind of QUADRUPLE time. But each beat is subdivided into three quavers. This makes it a COMPOUND time signature:

12/8 = COMPOUND QUADRUPLE

1 2 3   4 5 6   7 8 9   10 11 12

1 and a 2 and a 3 and a 4 and a

The COMPOUND QUADRUPLE metre gives the music a LIVELY, SWUNG feeling.

Show That You Know #1
The unique sound of this track depends on GUITAR EFFECTS and OVERDUBBING.

Show That You Know #2
The song has a VERSE-CHORUS structure, but some phrases are LOPSIDED in length.

Show That You Know #3
Compared to other popular songs, the HARMONIC LANGUAGE is quite RICH.

Show That You Know #4
SYNCOPATION + COMPOUND QUADRUPLE metre = LIVELY feel.

Show That You Know #5
A few notes before the first beat of the bar are called a PICK-UP or ANACRUSIS.

Show That You Know #6
This is as much about the FLASHY GUITAR as about the virtuosic SINGING.

Show That You Know #7
Not using a SYNTHESIZER was unusual for GLAM ROCK music of this period.

Show That You Know #8
The REPEAT AND FADE OUTRO is characteristic of 1970s' popular music.

Schwartz: 'Defying Gravity' from *Wicked* (2003)

LESSON 9

Who Is STEPHEN SCHWARTZ?

Schwartz is a major American composer of musical theatre. His other works include *Pippin*, *Godspell* and *The Magic Show*. He has also collaborated on Disney films like *Pocahontas*.

What is WICKED?

The musical *Wicked* is a retelling of the story of the Wizard of Oz, from the point of view of the Wicked Witch of the West, ELPHABA. The song 'Defying Gravity' is the Act One Finale. The end of Act One is usually a moment of high drama!

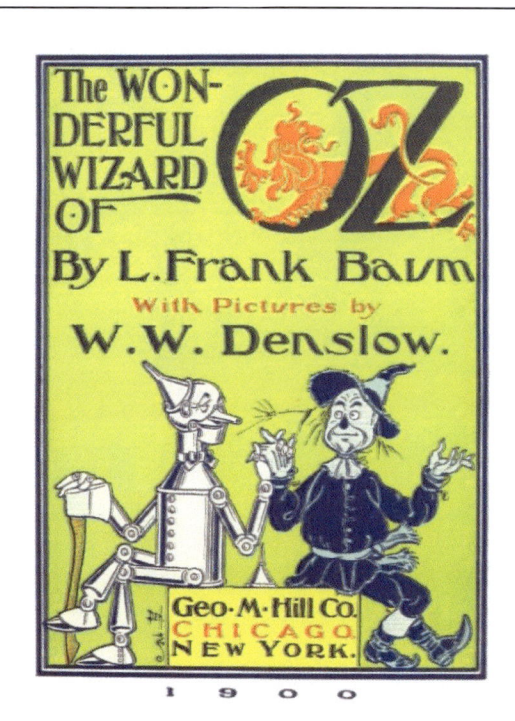

What's the TEXTURE?

Nearly always HOMOPHONIC, because there's nearly always a clear tune with a chordal accompaniment. There is some brief unaccompanied singing at the start, which is technically MONOPHONIC. Sometimes the two singers sing in UNISON. Your go-to answer about texture here is that it's HOMOPHONIC.

How Are DRAMATIC FEATURES Used In This Piece of Musical Theatre?

This song is characteristic of an ACT ONE FINALE, full of dramatic features and effects. Here's the checklist:

- ☑ Includes SPOKEN DIALOGUE
- ☑ Uses a WIDE VOCAL RANGE
- ☑ CHROMATIC STABS
- ☑ Large MELODIC LEAPS
- ☑ Full range of DYNAMICS
- ☑ Frequent use of SYNCOPATION
- ☑ DRIVING OSTINATO FIGURES
- ☑ Dramatic INSTRUMENTAL TECHNIQUES such as OVERDRIVE, TREMOLANDO and ROLL
- ☑ Verse 3 returns at the HIGHER OCTAVE
- ☑ Use of FULL BAND
- ☑ Inclusion of ANGRY CHORUS in RICH CHORDS at end.

GLINDA ...

... is the 'GOOD' WITCH. She is sung by a SOPRANO. Her role in this song is less demanding than Elphaba's (but she has more challenging music in other songs).

"You can still be with the wizard"

Her music in this song uses mainly simple, gentle CONJUNCT movement.

The Essential Knowledge Organiser

Who's Playing What?

TRADITIONAL CLASSICAL INSTRUMENTS are used. These include flute, oboe, bass clarinet, bassoon, two French horns, two trumpets, two trombones, harp, two violins, a viola, a cello, a double bass, and percussion.

POP/ROCK INSTRUMENTS are also used. These include baritone saxophone, drumkit, two electric guitars, and three electronic keyboards.

The **THREE ELECTRONIC KEYBOARDS** play an important role, filling out the sound and giving the impression of a much larger ensemble. They mostly play string and brass **PATCHES**.

EFFECTS like **OVERDRIVE** (on the guitar), **TREMOLANDO** (strings), **ROLL** (on cymbal) are used to create excitement. **UNUSUAL PERCUSSION INSTRUMENTS** such as **TUBULAR BELLS** are also added for extra dramatic effect.

There is also a **CHORUS** of singers, called '**ENSEMBLE**' on the score.

ELPHABA …

… is the '**WICKED' WITCH**. She is sung by a **MEZZO-SOPRANO**. Her role is vocally demanding, including the requirement to **BELT** high notes.

"It's time to try defying gravity"

Her music uses both **CONJUNCT** and **DISJUNCT** motion, and is often quite **ANGULAR**.

What's the Structure?

'Defying Gravity' has a **VERSE-CHORUS** structure:

INTRO — "I hope you're happy …"
VERSE 1 — "Something had changed within me …"
CHORUS — "It's time to try *defying gravity* …"
VERSE 2 — "I'm through accepting limits …"
CHORUS — "I'd sooner try *defying gravity* …"
BRIDGE — "Unlimited, together we're unlimited …"
CHORUS — "Just you and I *defying gravity* …"
REPEAT OF INTRO (with changes) — "I hope you're happy …"
VERSE 3 (at a higher octave) — "So if you care to find me …"
CHORUS — "Tell them how I'm *defying gravity* …"
CODA — "And nobody in all of Oz …"

Schwartz: 'Defying Gravity' from *Wicked* (2003)

LESSON 10

What If I'm Asked to Describe the VOCAL WRITING or the MELODIC FEATURES?

"I hope you're happy! I hope you're happy now!" (bars 1 to 3) → RECITATIVE (speech-style singing) in free time without very much accompaniment.

Lots of SYNCOPATION (notes falling between the beats) which creates movement and excitement. → "Something has changed within me, Something is not the same" (bars 34 to 37)

"I'm through with playing by the rules of someone else's game." (bars 38 to 41) → Large vocal LEAPS (here between 'the' and 'rules') show Elphaba's confidence.

Move to the HIGHER OCTAVE and punchy ACCENTUATION create excitement. → Verse 3: "So if you care to find me, look to the Western sky" (bars 135 to 138)

"It's time to try defying gravity" (bars 50 to 53) → A really catchy HOOK on 'defying gravity'.

The vocal writing is always SYLLABIC, so this is always a good answer to vocal writing questions!

What's the TONALITY?

'Defying Gravity' is mostly in D MAJOR. It has a brief G MAJOR section, bars 88 to 100. (Watch how the C sharp vanishes.)

Schwartz moves through different keys in sections like bars 20 to 32, which is typical of MUSICAL THEATRE WRITING.

The only moments of less clear tonality are at the very start and in bars 115 to 131 where Schwartz uses CHROMATIC writing.

How About the HARMONY?

Generally conventional harmonies and chords used throughout. Schwartz sometimes uses 'SUS' CHORDS, which create tension by adding a clashing note to a 'normal' triad.

Example:

In bar 60, $Gsus^2$ chord includes G-A-D notes instead of the usual G-B-D.

What Are Those PERFORMANCE INDICATIONS All About?

"COLLA VOCE" = literally "with the voice", meaning that the instruments must follow the singer's rhythm.

"TUTTI" = literally "everyone", meaning that the whole band is playing this part.

"TREMOLANDO" = a kind of shaking effect, where a note is played repeatedly.

"RALL" = getting slower.

"A TEMPO" = back to original speed.

"MAESTOSO" = majestic.

sfz = a strong, sudden accent.

"OVERDRIVE" = a guitar pedal effect similar to distortion, which creates a sound from rock music.

How Does Schwartz Create CONTRAST?

- ☑ Massive DYNAMIC RANGE, from *pp* to *ff*.
- ☑ Contrasting VOCAL WRITING for the soloists.
- ☑ An extended VERSE-CHORUS structure.
- ☑ Varied ACCOMPANIMENT PATTERNS.
- ☑ Using various INSTRUMENTAL EFFECTS.
- ☑ Combining TRADITIONAL CLASSICAL instruments with POP/ROCK INSTRUMENTS.

What Are the Important MOTIFS and MELODIC IDEAS?

MAIN MELODIC IDEA for the orchestral music. Chordal with rising bass line. First heard in bar 20.

"ELPHABA'S THEME", heard throughout *Wicked*. Matches the words 'Defying Gravity'. First heard in bar 21.

'UNLIMITED' THEME

Comes from the first seven notes of 'Somewhere over the rainbow' from the musical *The Wizard of Oz*.

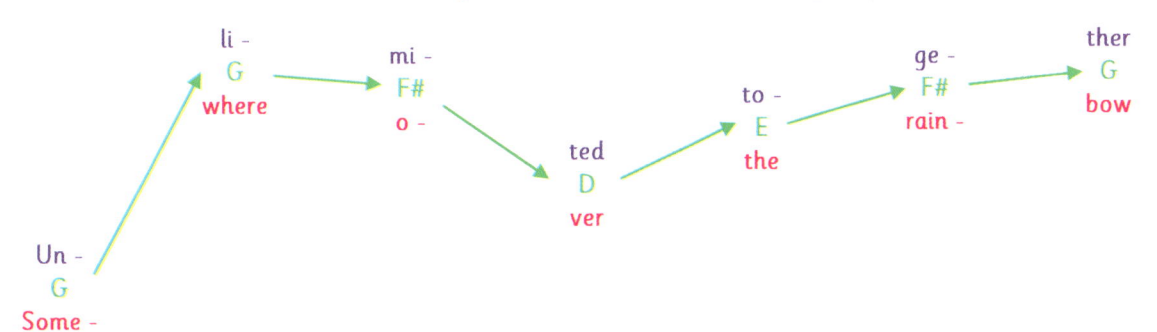

	li- G where	mi- F# o-	ted D ver	to- E the	ge- F# rain-	ther G bow
Un- G Some-						

OSTINATO ideas are used often to create magic, drama and excitement. Examples in bars 51 to 58, 80 to 86, 99 to 99, 103 to 109, and 152 to 160.

Edexcel GCSE Music Exam

John Williams: 'Main Title' / 'Rebel Blockade Runner' from Star Wars (1977)

LESSON 11

Who Is JOHN WILLIAMS?

Williams is the pre-eminent Hollywood film composer of his generation. His film scores include *Superman*, *Indiana Jones*, *Home Alone*, *Schindler's List*, *Jurassic Park* and *Harry Potter*.

(Not to be confused with the classical guitarist of the same name ...)

What's STAR WARS?

A battle between GOOD and EVIL set in space. Its themes and setting are very much linked with the music of this set work: WAR / MILITARY, HEROISM, LOVE, the COSMOS.

GEORGE LUCAS directed the 1977 film, going on to develop a worldwide pop-culture phenomenon, various other films, TV series, video games, theme park rides and comic books.

Star Wars is one of the HIGHEST-EARNING MEDIA FRANCHISES of all time.

How Does Williams Do EXCITEMENT?

Dramatic Dynamics

Ascending Melodic Leaps

(Like an upwards, heroic jump!)

Military Ostinato figures

(Featuring insistent triplet patterns)

Dissonance

(Strong harmonic clashes that attract attention)

TEXTURE

Mainly HOMOPHONIC, usually with a clear melody accompanied in various different ways by the orchestra. HOMOPHONIC is your go-to answer for texture questions here.

METRE

Strong 4/4 metre = SIMPLE QUADRUPLE.

Think about the march-like quality. It has to be in 4 or 2 otherwise you can't march to it.

INSTRUMENTAL FORCES

This is scored for a traditional LARGE SYMPHONY ORCHESTRA.

This means LOTS OF BRASS and LOTS OF DIFFERENT PERCUSSION. If you need an example of percussion, think about the 'Twinkling Stars' section, which uses CELESTE and XYLOPHONE.

Don't forget to mention that there are NO ELECTRONIC INSTRUMENTS here!

The Essential Knowledge Organiser

How Does Williams Do FANFARES?

Military-Sounding Triplets

Quartal Harmonies

(Chords made up of 'fourths' rather than 'thirds')

Use of Brass Instruments

(Trumpets, Trombones, French horns, Tubas)

What Signatures of JOHN WILLIAMS'S STYLE Are Heard in This Piece?

This work features all the characteristic **WILLIAMS "FINGERPRINTS"**.
Here's the checklist:

- ☑ **BRASS FANFARES**.
- ☑ **SOARING VIOLIN** melodies.
- ☑ **TRIUMPHANT MARCHES**.
- ☑ **HUGE SYMPHONY ORCHESTRA**.
- ☑ Use of **LEITMOTIFS**.
- ☑ Use of a **RICH HARMONIC LANGUAGE**.

What's the STRUCTURE?

The first half is led by **MUSICAL IDEAS** while the titles scroll:

Brass Fanfare
Heroic A Section
Contrasting, lyrical B Section
Return of heroic A Section

But the second half is led by **WHAT'S ON SCREEN**:

'Twinkling Stars'
'Huge Planet Appears'
'Small Spacecraft Under Attack'

What's the TONALITY?

The first half is DIATONIC and clearly in B FLAT MAJOR.

The second half becomes *less* clearly DIATONIC. It becomes increasingly ATONAL in the space-inspired section.

Finally, it becomes BITONAL (combining two keys) in the military sequence in the final ten bars.

Edexcel GCSE Music Exam

John Williams: 'Main Title' / 'Rebel Blockade Runner' from Star Wars (1977)

LESSON 12

The FIRST HALF Opens With a FANFARE

BARS 1 to 3

- Quartal Harmonies
- Use of Brass
- Loud Dynamics
- Military Triplets

The HEROIC A SECTION ("Luke Leitmotif") follows

BARS 4 to 11

- Ascending Leaps
- Syncopated Accompaniment
- Clear March-Like Metre

The LYRICAL B SECTION provides dramatic contrast

BARS 12 to 20

- Soaring Violins
- Conjunct Movement
- Chordal Accompaniment
- Calmer Accompaniment

Then the HEROIC A SECTION returns in an adapted form

BARS 21 to 29

INDICATIONS

+8va
Notes at higher octave also played.

Poco rall.
Slow down a little bit.

Tutti
Full orchestra playing.

A tempo
Back to the original speed.

Rit.
Slow down gradually.

Timp.
Short for timpani, or kettle drums.

Hrp. Gliss.
Glissando (a slide or sweep) on the harp.

Pizz.
String instruments pluck instead of using bow.

Celli
Plural of cello.

8va - - - - -
Plays an octave higher.

Cresc.
Crescendo. Gradually gets louder.

The Essential Knowledge Organiser

The SECOND HALF Returns to the FANFARE

BARS 30 to 32

Quartal Harmonies
Use of Brass
Loud Dynamics
Military Triplets

It passes through a **CHROMATIC REALM** before moving to the '**TWINKLING STARS**' moment

BARS 33 to 38

High Pitches
Metallic Instruments
Piccolo Solo
Short Detached Sounds

The **MASSIVE PLANET**'s appearance

BARS 39 to 50

Frantic Strings
Dramatic Brass Crescendo
Dissonance

The **SPACESHIP**'s appearance

BARS 51 to 60

Military Ostinato
Relentless Triplets
Bitonal Effect

Good Thing to Mention #1

Williams uses a very traditional, rich, **LATE-ROMANTIC MUSICAL LANGUAGE**.

Good Thing to Mention #2

He uses the film's themes to shape the music: **MILITARY**, **HEROISM** and **SPACE**.

Good Thing to Mention #3

Dissonance is crucial. Think **CHORD CLUSTERS** and **BITONAL** effects at end.

Good Thing to Mention #4

Try to mention the **CONTRASTS** between the **HEROIC A** and **LYRICAL B** sections.

Good Thing to Mention #5

Williams uses **LEITMOTIFS** associated with people, things or ideas: e.g. "Luke" theme.

Good Thing to Mention #6

The **STRUCTURE** is led by what's on the screen, especially after the "title scroll".

Good Thing to Mention #7

The instruments chosen for the 'Twinkling Stars' section create an **EERIE SOUND**.

Good Thing to Mention #8

PEDAL NOTES (e.g. at the end) and **INVERTED PEDAL NOTES** (opening) used.

Edexcel GCSE Music Exam

'Release' (from *Volume 2: Release*) by Afro Celt Sound System

LESSON 13

Why's This a FUSION? The CLUE IS IN THE NAME

AFRO – CELT – SOUND SYSTEM

African Influences · Celtic (esp. Irish) Influences · Techniques of Electronic Dance Music

---

From Africa …	From Celtic culture …	From EDM …
African instruments (see p. 30)	Celtic instruments (see p. 30)	EDM instruments (see p. 30)
Introduction spoken in the **Maninka language** of Guinea	Verse 2 sung in the **Irish Language**	Verses 1 and 3 sung in the **English language**
Structure that **emphasises repetition**	Triplet rhythms (characteristic of Irish folk music)	**Digital effects** (loops, panning)
Syncopation	**Aeolian mode**	Use of **electronic samples**
Polyrhythmic effects	Strings of short, rapid notes	Continuous tempo of **100 BPM**

What's the STRUCTURE?

Essentially a **STROPHIC** form (based on verses) with an **INTRO**, **SOLO SECTION** and an **OUTRO**.

INTRO	VERSE 1	VERSE 2	SOLOS	VERSE 3	BUILD	OUTRO
Drone + effects. Talking drum + spoken samples. Loops enter	Female vocalist sings in English. Loops accompany	Male vocalist sings in Irish. Loops accompany	Uilleann pipes. Low whistle. Hurdy-gurdy	Female vocalist sings in English. Loops accompany	Long crescendo. Drum break. Loops accompany	Female vocalist ('Reach out…') repeats phrase and fades with loops

African Instruments

- Kora
- Djembe 
- Talking Drum 

Celtic Instruments

- Fiddle
- Uilleann Pipes 
- Low Whistle 
- Bodhrán 
- Accordion 
- Hurdy-Gurdy 

Electronic Instruments

- Synthesizer
- Drum Machine 
- Electric Piano 

What's the METRE?

The **INTRODUCTION** is in free time.

After that the music has a clear four beats in the bar and moves at a **LIVELY TEMPO**.

4/4 = **SIMPLE QUADRUPLE**

What's the TEXTURE?

Mainly **HOMOPHONIC**, with a clear **TUNE** and **ACCOMPANIMENT**.

The **ACCOMPANIMENT** is made of **LOOPS** which are **LAYERED** on top of one another.

What's the MELODY like?

- ☑ **MODAL** – in the **AEOLIAN MODE**, specifically.
- ☑ Highly **REPETITIVE**.
- ☑ Mainly **CONJUNCT**.
- ☑ Mostly **SYLLABIC**.
- ☑ **FAIRLY LOW** in the vocal range.

What's that Long-Drawn-Out Sound?

That'll be a **DRONE**.

The drone on C keeps the piece firmly based on that main note.

What Effects (FX) Are Used?

- ☑ **REVERB**. Added to give the impression of a boomy, echoey acoustic.
- ☑ **PANNING**. Using stereo recording to place an instrument more to one speaker (or headphone) than the other.
- ☑ **SAMPLING**. Small extracts of recordings from real life or from other pieces of music brought in to the composition.
- ☑ Synthesizer **PADS**. These create impression of many string instruments.

Edexcel GCSE Music Exam

'Release' (from *Volume 2: Release*) by Afro Celt Sound System

LESSON 14

Section (Timings)	Main Features	Loops that First Appear
Intro (Beginning to 1.38)	Track opens with a drone (various effects including panning) Talking drum solo (not in score) Vocal samples (African language)	Loop 1 (bodhrán) Loop 2 (shaker) Loop 3 (drums) Loop 4 (synth) Loop 5 (drums)
Verse 1 (1.38 to 2.55)	Female vocalist enters ('Don't argue amongst yourselves ...', sung by Sinéad O'Connor in English) Loops accompany the solo, some dropping out, others beginning	Loop 6 (drums) Loop 7 (tambourine) Loop 8 (talking drum) Loop 9 (kora) Loop 10 (synth strings) Loop 11 (soft synth pad) Loop 12 (bass) Loop 13 (breath samples)
Verse 2 (2.55 to 3.51)	Punchy bass loop begins Male vocalist enters (singing in Irish) Loops accompany the solo, some dropping out, others beginning	Loop 14 (drums) Loop 15 (fiddle)
Solos (3.51 to 4.55)	Solo on uilleann pipes (Fig. 5) Solo on low whistle (Fig. 6) Solo on hurdy gurdy (Loop 20)	Loop 16 (synth) Loop 17 (accordion) Loop 18 (bodhrán) Loop 19 (male vox = voice) Loop 20 (hurdy gurdy) Loop 21 (synth pad)
Verse 3 (4.55 to 5.51)	Another Sinéad O'Connor solo ('Don't argue amongst yourselves ...') Solos from hurdy gurdy and uilleann pipes Loops accompany the solo, some dropping out, others beginning	Loop 22 (synth) Loop 23 (fiddle)
Drum break, build (5.51 to 6.59)	Lively drum break (Loop 24) Electric piano builds the excitement (Loops 25 & 26)	Loop 24 (drums) Loop 25 (electric piano) Loop 26 (electric piano) Loop 27 (hurdy gurdy) Loop 28 (uilleann pipes)
Outro (6.59 to 7.28)	Female vocalist ('Reach out and touch me') Loops Song fades	No new loops

The Essential Knowledge Organiser

Some VOCABULARY and INDICATIONS

VOX
Another word for voice or voices.

UILLEANN
Pronounced 'ILL-un'. Irish language word meaning 'elbow', which is where this instrument is played.

LOOP
Short, digitally repeated passage.

+8va
At an octave one higher than is written.

GLISS.
Slide from one note to the next as shown by the line.

Did I Mention? #1
This piece includes influences from AFRICAN, CELTIC and EDM cultures.

Did I Mention? #2
CHOICE OF INSTRUMENTS is a clear way in which the three cultures are represented.

Did I Mention? #3
The structure is STROPHIC.

Did I Mention? #4
A range of different ELECTRONIC TECHNIQUES and EFFECTS is used.

Did I Mention? #5
The track includes three languages: MANINKA, IRISH and ENGLISH.

Did I Mention? #6
Layering different rhythmic loops on top of one another creates POLYRHYTHM.

Did I Mention? #7
The use of LOOPS & DRONES means that this track has very STATIC HARMONIES.

Did I Mention? #8
The female vocalist is the famous Irish singer-songwriter SINÉAD O'CONNOR.

31

Edexcel GCSE Music Exam

'Samba Em Prelúdio' performed by Esperanza Spalding

LESSON 15

Who Wrote This?

The Brazilian guitarist Roberto Baden Powell de Aquino wrote the music and Vinícius de Moraes wrote the lyric. The song was written in 1962.

Who Performs This?

Esperanza Spalding (b. 1984). Bassist, singer, multi-instrumentalist. American virtuoso musician and Grammy Award winner. She released 'Samba Em Prelúdio' in 2008.

What's the Structure?

Basically STROPHIC (in verses) as follows:

INTRODUCTION
Acoustic bass only. Bars 1 to 3.

VERSE 1
MELODY A is played twice (bars 4 to 11, then 12 to 18). This section finishes with four bars of 'bossa' rhythm (bars 19 to 22). Just voice and acoustic bass.

VERSE 2
MELODY B is played twice (first, bars 23 to 38, then varied a bit in bars 39 to 54). Voice, acoustic bass and acoustic guitar.

Virtuosic GUITAR SOLO based on MELODY B.

VERSE 3 combines an AUGMENTED version of MELODY A in the bass with sung MELODY B. Acoustic guitar silent. Then bars 39 to 54 again.

CODA based on part of MELODY B.

Short version:
Intro-AA¹-BB¹-Solo-Repeats-Coda

What's the METRE?

4/4 = SIMPLE QUADRUPLE

What's the TONALITY?

B MINOR with JAZZ HARMONIES, capturing the mood of LOST LOVE

What's the TEXTURE?

ALL THREE textures appear!
See more on p. 34.

Why Is This a FUSION?

Because <u>SAMBA</u> + <u>COOL JAZZ</u> = <u>BOSSA NOVA</u>!

<u>BOSSA NOVA</u> is a style that emerged in the late 1950s and early 1960s in Rio de Janeiro. Some people think of it as a <u>MODERNISATION</u> of the samba style.

Its vibe is characteristically <u>LAID BACK</u> and <u>LILTING</u>.

It is a <u>BRAZILIAN</u> tradition, sung in <u>PORTUGUESE</u>.

Its themes are <u>LOVE</u>, <u>LONGING</u>, <u>HOMESICKNESS</u> and <u>NATURE</u>.

What SAMBA FEATURES are heard in this piece?

This work includes characteristic <u>SAMBA FEATURES</u>.

<u>SAMBA</u> is a Brazilian style that shares many musical characteristics of the <u>LATIN CULTURES</u> of <u>CENTRAL AMERICAN</u>, <u>SOUTH AMERICAN</u> and the <u>CARIBBEAN</u>.

Here's the SAMBA FEATURES checklist:

- ☑ <u>BOSSA NOVA RHYTHM</u>, with its distinctive <u>SYNCOPATED, LATIN VIBE</u> (this kicks in at bar 19).
- ☑ <u>VIRTUOSIC GUITAR</u> playing, using both <u>FINGER-PICKING</u> and <u>STRUMMING</u> techniques.
- ☑ Often written as a <u>DANCE</u>.
- ☑ Includes <u>SINGING</u>.

What COOL JAZZ FEATURES are heard in this piece?

As a <u>BOSSA NOVA</u> rather than a true <u>SAMBA</u>, this piece also shows characteristic features of <u>COOL JAZZ</u>. Here's the checklist:

- ☑ <u>JAZZ HARMONIES</u> including <u>SEVENTH CHORDS</u> and other <u>EXTENDED CHORDS</u>, giving the music a sophisticated feel.
- ☑ Expressive <u>ALTERED CHORDS</u>.
- ☑ An unhurried, <u>LAID-BACK TEMPO</u>.
- ☑ Lots of <u>RUBATO</u>, where the tempo of the music slows down and speeds up for expressive purposes.
- ☑ <u>SYNCOPATION</u> (which is, as you can see above, also a main feature of the samba style).
- ☑ Prominent <u>IMPROVISATORY INSTRUMENTAL SOLOS</u>.

What Instruments and Voices Do We Hear?

<u>FEMALE VOICE</u> – low <u>TESSITURA</u> (pitch range).

<u>ACOUSTIC BASS GUITAR</u> – a four-stringed instrument shown in picture above. See next page for the characteristic ways this is played.

<u>ACOUSTIC GUITAR</u> (six strings) joining at bar 23. Mainly plays chords and melodic fragments, but has a <u>VIRTUOSIC SOLO</u> in the middle of the piece.

Edexcel GCSE Music Exam

'Samba Em Prelúdio' performed by Esperanza Spalding
LESSON 16

What Can We Say About TEXTURE?

This song is mainly **HOMOPHONIC** because it has a main tune that is accompanied. (Sometimes the tune appears in two octaves at once – that's still homophonic). There are some significant exceptions:

The opening of the song is **MONOPHONIC**, since there is a single line playing unaccompanied (bars 1 to 3). This texture also appears in the acoustic guitar solo passage between **VERSES 2 and 3**.

There are some moments of **POLYPHONIC TEXTURE**, where, for example, the acoustic bass guitar and vocal lines combine Melodies A and B (bars 88 to 103).

And if this passage gets mentioned, don't forget to say that the bass guitar's line is **AUGMENTED** (played in note values of twice the normal length).

Your go-to answer is to say that a VARIETY of different textures is used!

MELODY 'A' vs. MELODY 'B'

A: Eu sem você não tenho porqê
Porque sem você não sei nem chorar (bars 4 to 7)
(Without you I'm aimless
Because without you, I can't even cry)

Melody 'A'. First heard at bar 4. It's based on a **DISJUNCT** ascending four-note figure. A spiky shape, with bursts of notes separated by rests.

B: Ai, que saudade
Que vontade de ver renascer nossa vida (from b. 23)
(Oh, what longing
A desire to see our life reborn)

Melody 'B'. First heard at bar 23. Almost entirely **CONJUNCT**, with a smoother, longer line, narrower range and fewer rests.

What's contrasting?
DISJUNCT & DISJOINTED vs. **CONJUNCT & LINEAR**.

What are the similarities? Both lines are entirely **SYLLABIC** settings.

You're Going to Try to Say … #1

"BOSSA NOVA! A fusion of features from SAMBA and COOL JAZZ!"

You're Going to Try to Say … #2

"Hey, look at those JAZZ CHORDS and HARMONIES, like SEVENTHS!"

The Essential Knowledge Organiser

What Are All Those Crazy CHORDS and HARMONIES?

It's a bit less complicated that it looks. You've got four categories: (1) <u>PLAIN OLD TRIADS</u>, (2) <u>SEVENTH</u> chords, (3) further <u>EXTENDED</u> chords, and (4) <u>ALTERED</u> chords.

In traditional harmony, most chords have three notes. We *rarely* hear this happening here. ↓

C⁷

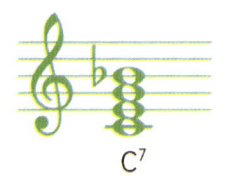

Extended chords like NINTH, ELEVENTH and THIRTEENTH chords just add more and more notes. ↓

G⁹#⁵

G chord, extended with a seventh and a ninth, but the fifth is sharpened! (G B D# F A)

C major

↑ In jazz harmony, many chords are SEVENTH chords, where an extra note, seven up from the root, is added to each chord.

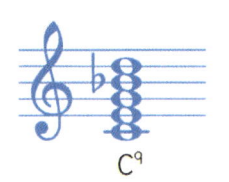

C⁹

↑ Take an extended chord, change one note by a semitone, and you've got a chromatic-sounding ALTERED CHORD.

<u>EXTENDED CHORDS</u> (including <u>SEVENTH CHORDS</u>) and <u>ALTERED CHORDS</u> are your go-to answers to questions about the <u>HARMONIC FEATURES</u> of this work! And don't forget to mention that there are very few <u>PLAIN TRIAD CHORDS</u>!

Features of the ACOUSTIC BASS GUITAR Part

The introduction of the whole song contains many of the major features:

Check out the first three bars and spot the following:

| MORDENT | DOUBLE-STOPPED chords: two notes played together | CHROMATIC movement based on SEMITONES | BUSY arpeggios | GLISSANDO, where player slides between notes. |
| SCALE patterns | | | HARMONICS | |

Your go-to answers about the <u>ACOUSTIC BASS GUITAR FEATURES</u> of this work are <u>VIRTUOSITY</u>, use of <u>HARMONICS</u>, writing based on <u>SCALES AND ARPEGGIOS</u> and the use of <u>DOUBLE-STOPS</u>.

You're Going to Try to Say … #3

"Hey, look at that VIRTUOSIC playing in the acoustic bass & acoustic guitar!"

You're Going to Try to Say … #4

"Hey, look at the very clever way MELODIES A and B get COMBINED!"

You're Going to Try to Say … #5

"Hey, look at how well the music captures the mood of the lyric!"

Printed in Great Britain
by Amazon